POST-STATE FUTURISM

BOOK I

FOUNDATIONS OF POST-STATE FUTURISM

A philosophical framework that challenges the underlying power structures of the modern state.

Jason Corgan Brown

Published by Corgan Studio Press

(424) 281-9847

www.corganstudio.com

"Foundations of Post-State Futurism" is Book I in an ongoing series exploring the conceptual groundwork of Post-State Futurism, a developing philosophical framework.

This work presents emerging philosophical ideas and is intended for educational, reflective, and conceptual purposes. All interpretations are the responsibility of the reader. This text outlines a developing conceptual framework and is not intended as political advice, legal guidance, or a prescriptive doctrine.

ISBN: 979-8-2954-2140-2

Library of Congress Control Number: 2025926721

First Edition: 2026

Cover design by Corgan Studio

Printed in the United States of America

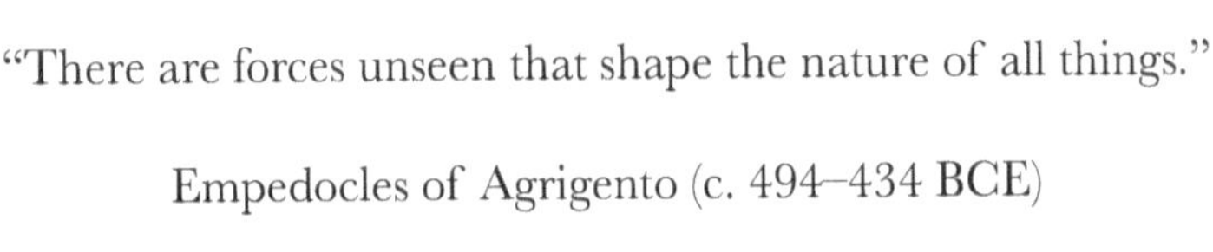

"There are forces unseen that shape the nature of all things."

Empedocles of Agrigento (c. 494–434 BCE)

CHAPTER I

The Unsettling Inheritance

WHERE THE STATE BEGINS AND THE HUMAN SELF ENDS

There are moments in every civilization when its people feel a subtle pressure in the air, a quiet but mistakable tension, as though the world they inherited is slightly out of tune with the world they feel inside themselves. These moments rarely erupt into revolution; more often they linger, like a soft hum beneath consciousness. Post-State Futurism begins here, at the hum, the uneasy vibration beneath the inherited architecture of political life.

For most of human history, people did not choose their governments; they were born into them. They did not imagine that political systems could be different, because their systems were as constant as the seasons, as immutable as the sky. The state was not an institution, it was an atmosphere.

To understand the state, one must begin with this atmospheric quality. The state enters the human mind long before the human mind can question it: flags before reason, pledges before doubt, borders before worldliness. The structure precedes the self. Identity is poured into a container that appears natural only because it has existed for generations.

But structures older than memory often hide origins that would destabilize their sanctity if remembered fully.

THE FIRST SHADOWS

The earliest states emerged not from philosopher-kings, nor from social
contracts, but from the cold arithmetic of force. Sedentary agriculture
produced both surplus and vulnerability. Surplus attracted plunder.
Vulnerability demanded protection. Protection required organization.
Organization required hierarchy. And hierarchy required a story: a story
that justified why some commanded and others obeyed.

That story, repeated long enough, becomes indistinguishable from truth.

Post-State Futurism does not moralize this origin; it dissects it. The project
is neither anarchic nor utopian, neither revolutionary nor reactionary. It is
diagnostic. It seeks to expose the deeper machinery that underlies political
identity, and the long shadow cast by the earliest bargains struck between
protection and obedience.

What we call the "state" is the descendant of these bargains. But the state
of today is not the state of antiquity; it is their perfected form — a system
that has learned not only to command bodies, but to cultivate the interior
landscapes of its subjects. The modern state governs the imagination as
much as the territory.

THE INVISIBLE CONTRACT

The foundations of political life rest on a paradox: the state presents itself
as the guarantor of order, yet its power arises from its monopoly on the
very violence it claims to protect us from. This contradiction is rarely
noticed because it is framed as common sense. The state protects, therefore
the state must rule. It rules, therefore it must be protected.

This looping justification forms the core of what Post-State Futurism calls the invisible contract: a contract never signed, never read, and never negotiable. It is inherited the moment one is born into a jurisdiction. The contract claims that identity flows from geography, that belonging flows from legal designation, and that loyalty flows from birth.

But inheritance is not the same as consent, and geography is not the same as destiny.

THE FIRST BOUNDARY: THE MIND

Before the state claims land, it claims the imagination. Children learn the map of their nation before they learn the meaning of mapping. They learn the anthem before they understand the meaning of ritual. They learn the myth of national origin before they learn the concept of myth.

This slow accumulation of symbolic material creates the illusion that the state is not an institution but a family. Dissent becomes betrayal not of a system, but of something more intimate: the imagined community that has fused itself with one's emotional reflexes.

STANDING AT THE THRESHOLD

To study the state from the outside, as if one were a traveler passing through a structure rather than a member living inside it, is to experience a fundamental reorientation. The walls that once felt like home reveal their architecture. The boundaries that once felt natural reveal their artificiality. The powers that once felt protective reveal their extraction.

Post-State Futurism begins at this threshold: the moment a person realizes that the world they inherited was not inevitable, and that political identity is not destiny but conditioning.

This chapter opens the first crack in the inherited foundation. The chapters that follow widen it.

CHAPTER II

The Deep Genealogy of Power

There are stories we tell about where the state came from, and then there are the stories beneath those stories: the sediment of human organization, compacted by centuries of coercion, fear, obedience, and the slow normalization of hierarchy. To understand the modern state, one must look not at constitutions, charters, or glorious founding myths, but at the ground beneath them: the fields of early wheat and barley, the river valleys where human beings first surrendered their wandering lives to the geometry of walls, granaries, and enumerated labor.

The genealogy of the state is not a genealogy of ideas. It is a genealogy of capture.

Long before any political philosopher imagined a social contract, long before kings invoked divine sanction, and long before bureaucrats invented civic identity, the earliest proto-states formed around a simple principle: grain could be counted, and what could be counted could be controlled.

The first rulers were not leaders of people, they were custodians of calories. They commanded the harvest not through inspiration, but through the architecture of storage. A granary is not a building. It is a device for organizing human life around what does not belong to them.

In these early enclosures, we witness the birth of legibility.

To govern, one must count.

To count, one must immobilize.

To immobilize, one must contain.

The early state learned each of these lessons slowly, across centuries, innovating coercion as naturally as a tree grows rings. Sedentary life expanded the possibilities of control. Fields replaced forests, and with them the unpredictable autonomy of wandering gave way to the predictable rhythms of agricultural labor. It was from these rhythms that rulers learned their craft: how to extract without exhausting, how to intimidate without inciting revolt, how to make obedience feel like an ordinary part of the seasons.

Power, once established, does not merely reproduce… it deepens.

It roots itself into the soil of memory and the rituals of daily existence.

THE RITUALIZATION OF FORCE

Early rulership was elemental. A blade, a threat, a demand. But even violence seeks efficiency. Constant repression is costly; it tires even the conqueror. Power needed a way to conserve itself.

And so, force became ritual.

The threatening gesture hardened into law.

The war cry softened into a proclamation.

The extortion became taxation, softened by the language of duty.

When warlords realized they could stabilize their extraction by making it predictable, "you owe me this much, every season, forever", the state moved from improvisation to permanence. Bureaucracy was born not as a strategy of fairness but as a technique for lowering the cost of domination.

A ledger is simply a weapon with better stamina.

THE INVENTION OF THE PERMANENT POPULATION

Before states existed, people moved. Movement is the oldest form of freedom. To move is to refuse capture. To move is to outrun a ruler's design.

This is why early states fixated on sedentarization. A population that moves cannot be taxed, monitored, or drafted. A population that moves lives outside the logic of hierarchy.

Thus the state's earliest project was to restrict motion.

Walls appeared: around cities, then around fields, then around the very notion of belonging. What was once a fluid landscape of tribes, families, and crossings became a grid of obligations, anchored by a center of power. To belong meant, increasingly, to remain.

The state emerges precisely when the population stops emerging.

Only then can power rest.

Only then can extraction stabilize.

Only then can the ruler sleep.

The Disappearance of the Initial Violence

As domination endures, it acquires a veneer.

Centuries pass.

People forget.

The brutal origins of the state soften into parable or patriotic nostalgia. What was once a conquest becomes "founding." What was once forced labor becomes "civilization." What was once a shackle becomes "duty." The state depends on this forgetting. It requires the population to inherit the structure without inheriting the memory.

This is the central trick of power:

If the origin cannot be justified, it must be obscured.

The genealogical truth becomes buried beneath the mythology of legitimacy. The sword becomes the scepter. The overseer becomes the magistrate. The enclosure becomes the homeland.

It is not that the violence vanished, it became atmospheric.

It became administrative.

It became expected.

Modern states no longer need to display coercion because they have perfected the art of making citizens perform the work of obedience for them.

THE EVOLUTION OF LEGIBILITY

To govern is to see.

To see is to measure.

To measure is to simplify.

Modern states inherited the ancient obsession with legibility and magnified it exponentially. Census-taking, land surveys, property records, identification papers, schooling, and standardization serve the same function as ancient granaries: they convert human lives into manageable units.

In this genealogy, the state's gaze becomes the most important organ of power. Once the population is visible in the way the state requires, not as complex beings but as taxable, trainable, mobilizable objects, the structure of control becomes nearly effortless.

People begin to anticipate what the state sees and adjust themselves accordingly.

This anticipatory obedience is the most refined form of domination.

THE DEEP LOGIC OF EXTRACTION

At every stage of its development, the state refines the same fundamental act: extracting value from the population by making that extraction feel normal.

In this light, the social contract is not a mutual agreement: it is a narrative innovation, a retroactive gloss on a coercive lineage.

The genealogy of the state is the genealogy of the siphon.

What changes over time is not the act of extraction, but the sophistication of its justification. Fear comes first, followed by ritual, then law. Identity is folded in later, then patriotism, then the appeal to economic necessity. The final claim is existential: without the state, everything collapses. At this stage of genealogical control, the population no longer experiences the state as power, but as life itself.

THE GENEALOGICAL BLIND SPOT

And yet, the original truth remains, hidden beneath all the layers of narrative:

The state did not arise because humans needed order.

The state arose because certain humans discovered that order could be used to control others.

Power preceded justification.

Extraction preceded ideology.

Domination preceded belonging.

The deep genealogy of the state is not a story of mutual agreement.

It is the story of how one group convinced another group that obedience was their inheritance.

THE CHAPTER'S CLOSING INSIGHT

To trace the genealogy of the state is to see through its disguises.

It is to understand that the institution we treat as inevitable is, in fact, a long shadow cast by ancient acts of capture.

The purpose of genealogy is not to condemn the state, nor to romanticize a world without it, but to clarify what has been forgotten:

The forms of power that shape us today were not designed for our benefit.

They were designed for the benefit of those who first learned how to enclose.

Once this is understood, the horizon of political possibility widens.

We begin to see that the state is not destiny, it is merely one historical configuration among many.

And what has been constructed can be reconstructed.

What has been normalized can be reimagined.

What has been inherited can be transcended.

CHAPTER III

The Macro-Syndicate

The modern state is often described using the polite vocabulary of civics: "institutions," "governance," "public service," "representation." These words smooth the contours of something far older and more primitive, something whose ancestral bones still protrude beneath the polished grammar of the present. States did not begin as visions; they began as consolidations. Not as ideals, but as monopolies. Not as collective dreams, but as controlled enclosures.

To understand the state is to trace the lineage of power back to its earliest form: the syndicate.

THE CONTINUITY OF DOMINATION

The first syndicates did not call themselves governments. They were clusters of armed men who discovered that fear could be harvested like grain. They learned that the threat of violence, once successfully imposed, required less and less demonstration over time. A village that resisted once would resist again; a village that submitted could be maintained with only a fraction of the original force.

Over time, these early enforcers realized that predictable extraction, of food, labor, or obedience, was more profitable than sporadic pillaging. The rhythm of domination shifted from raid to rule, from plunder to taxation, from spectacle to structure.

What began as extortion grew into administration.

This continuity is not metaphorical; it is structural.

The modern state still extracts, still disciplines, still enforces territory. Only the methods have become less visible, diffused into law, culture, bureaucracy, and emotional belonging. The sword has become subtler but not less sharp.

The macro-syndicate is what the syndicate becomes when it learns to inherit itself.

FROM WARLORD TO BUREAUCRAT

The warlord's tools were concrete: a blade, a fire, a boundary drawn by force. His authority lasted only as long as his strength. Over generations, power discovered its most effective strategy: to escape the mortality of the individual by attaching itself to ritual.

The warlord hardens into a dynasty. The dynasty stabilizes as an administration. The administration formalizes into a state, until the state itself becomes ambient, no longer experienced as an actor but as an atmosphere.

As this syndicate evolves, coercion refines its instruments. The sword reappears as law. Tribute is reorganized as taxation. Loyalty is professionalized into civil service. Territory is abstracted into borders. Even threat is laundered into curriculum.

Nothing essential changes. Only the form improves.

LEGITIMACY AS A TECHNOLOGY

For the early syndicate, legitimacy was irrelevant. Victory was sufficient. But victory decays unless it is ritualized. The first rulers to survive beyond memory were those who learned to present their dominance not as superiority, but as inevitability. Authority was attached to gods, to soil, to myth, to seasonal cycles that appeared older and more permanent than any individual ruler. Over centuries, these performances hardened into legitimacy, a technology as effective as force and far more durable.

The modern state, inheritor of this lineage, perfects legitimacy by embedding it everywhere. Education teaches identity as destiny. Ceremony converts obedience into belonging. Narrative reframes taxation as contribution. Borders transform containment into meaning. Law itself rebrands coercion as order. Violence no longer needs to be visible to function.

Legitimacy is the form of violence that draws no blood.

A syndicate survives only as long as its enforcers can impose their will. A macro-syndicate survives because the population internalizes that will instead. The administrative state does not coerce every citizen individually; it engineers the conditions under which citizens learn to coerce themselves. This is the secret of multi-generational power: the fusion of personal identity with system identity. When a child learns to salute a flag before understanding the structure the flag represents, the syndicate approaches immortality.

A successful state does not merely dominate. It becomes familiar.

It does not merely regulate. It becomes normal.

It does not merely survive. It becomes unquestioned.

THE SCALE OF THE MACRO-SYNDICATE

The macro-syndicate differs from its early forms not by abandoning coercion, but by scaling and stabilizing it. Where its predecessors ruled dozens, it governs millions. Where their power lasted seasons, its authority persists for centuries. Territory is no longer held through constant patrol, but defined and enforced through law. Extraction becomes financialized, institutionalized, and automated. Narrative embeds itself in memory, culture, and identity, while compliance is no longer extorted through fear but volunteered as self-description.

Because of this, the macro-syndicate does not need to reassert itself through daily violence. The population, shaped by generational conditioning, reproduces the system through assumptions, emotions, and inherited loyalties. The state's greatest achievement is not the erasure of its origins in coercion, but the refinement of their invisibility.

THE HIDDEN ARCHITECTURE OF POWER

If one examines the bureaucratic structures of the modern state—its ministries, courts, taxation offices, border systems, and law-enforcement hierarchies—what appears is a monumental architecture built atop primitive foundations. Every form, every permit, every regulation still carries the faint shadow of the sword that once enforced it.

Coercion has not disappeared. It has been translated. Policy replaces command. Procedure replaces threat. Necessity replaces justification. Patriotism replaces fear. Where ancient power ruled through immediate violence, modern power governs by shaping the psychological climate in which choices are made.

The state becomes a controlled horizon when its limits grow indistinguishable from the edges of thought.

THE MACRO-SYNDICATE'S MASK

The great paradox of the state is that it gains strength by pretending it is not a syndicate. By calling itself democracy, it conceals extraction. By calling itself nation, it conceals containment. By calling itself civilization, it conceals inheritance.

The mask does not negate the structure; it completes it.

A syndicate capable of ruling without violence is stronger than one that depends upon it.

A population that believes obedience is identity does not need to be forced.

The macro-syndicate is not the opposite of government; it is the hidden truth beneath it.

CHAPTER IV

The Architecture of Obedience

Obedience does not begin with law.

Law arrives late, after the internal terrain has already been surveyed, softened, and prepared.

Before a state can command the body, it must first persuade the mind that command is reasonable, necessary, even natural.

Every political order begins as a choreography of attention.

The child learns early what is worth noticing and what must be ignored.

He absorbs the symbols before he comprehends their purpose.

A flag is not yet a history, a nation, or a claim: it is simply a shape in the corner of the classroom.

Yet every morning it rises like a minor sun, and every morning a room of unformed citizens aligns themselves toward it.

The ritual is small, almost invisible, but it carries the future in its hands.

Over time, the citizen learns to stand not because he chooses to, but because standing has become part of the body's inherited grammar.

This is the first structure of obedience: habituation.

Obedience as muscle memory.

RITUAL AS SOFT COERCION

Ritual is where a state first enters the private interior of a person.

It creates rhythms, seasons, and shared emotional climates.

Holidays lacquer the past.

Ceremonies distribute meaning.

Loss is framed collectively.

Victory is celebrated collectively.

Even grief becomes a public instrument.

The state does not demand belief.

It demands rhythm.

Once the rhythm is established, belief follows automatically because it becomes exhausting not to follow it.

Most political power is exercised this way, through the comfort of repetition.

THE INVISIBLE CURRICULUM

Schools do not teach political theory; they teach a political lens. Before a child encounters the world directly, the state offers a world already interpreted. Borders are presented as natural lines. Wars are framed as moral narratives. National character is treated as destiny. Governance recedes into the background, experienced not as a construct but as the condition of life itself.

The invisible curriculum is not the content being taught, but the frame that renders that content self-evident. This is why states do not fear illiteracy as much as they fear alternative literacy, ways of reading the world that do not pass through their grammar. A population may be educated or uneducated and remain obedient, so long as the frame holds. It is only when the frame fractures that obedience begins to fail.

THE SEDUCTION OF STABILITY

The state's power rests not only on coercion, but on its promise of predictability. Humans crave continuity as deeply as they crave freedom, and often more. The architecture of obedience is built to exploit this tension. When the state presents itself as the guarantor of order, the vessel of continuity, and the neutral organizer of life, dissent quietly transforms. It is no longer experienced as a political act, but as a personal risk.

Inside the citizen, a question replaces conviction: if I pull away from the structure, will the structure pull away from me? Obedience becomes a form of emotional risk management. The citizen complies not because the state is loved, but because the alternative feels like standing alone in the wind, without walls.

THE BENEVOLENT MASK

Every regime coats its authority in the language of virtue. Even the most extractive systems describe themselves as protective, stabilizing, and necessary. Obedience is easiest to cultivate when power adopts the posture of care, appears reluctant to govern, and claims to carry heavy burdens on behalf of the people.

When domination presents itself as guardianship, submission is internalized as gratitude. Obedience no longer needs to be enforced from the outside. It becomes ambient. A benign face is the most cost-effective instrument of control.

SELF-SURVEILLANCE

When the state succeeds in embedding its categories, myths, and emotional contours into a population, governance becomes self-executing. The citizen begins to function as an extension of the state's sensory apparatus, reporting deviations, enforcing norms, absorbing punishment without rebellion, and apologizing for thoughts that fall outside the approved frame.

The greatest victory of any power structure is reached when the governed actively defend the architecture of their own subordination. At this point, punishment no longer needs to be imposed from above. The population administers it internally. Obedience becomes self-sustaining.

THE QUIET WEIGHT OF INHERITED REALITY

The state's architecture of obedience is not a machine built atop people; it is a machine built within them.

Its walls are assumptions.

Its foundations are habits.

Its ceilings are the limits of imagination.

The most powerful political structure is not the army, the legislature, or the constitution, it is the citizen who cannot conceive of life outside the state, who sees the walls of the system as the edges of the world.

States do not endure because they are strong.

They endure because their populations are trained to imagine no alternative.

THE TURNING POINT

The architecture of obedience persists until a threshold is reached:

when awareness finally seeps into the conditioned spaces of thought and reveals the invisible conduits of influence.

At that moment, a person does not become an enemy of the state, he becomes a foreigner in his own inherited reality.

He steps outside the slow choreography and begins to perceive:

not what the state says

but how the state says it,

not what obedience requires

but how obedience is constructed.

This is the beginning of political consciousness:

the first fracture in the interior architecture.

And once a structure cracks, its silhouette becomes visible.

CHAPTER V

The Machinery of Obedience

Obedience is often described as a response, a reaction to authority — but in truth it is something far more intricate, far more deeply cultivated. No state survives simply by commanding. It survives by shaping the internal terrain of its people until command becomes unnecessary. Obedience, in its perfected form, is not demanded but offered.

In this sense, obedience is not the visible mechanism of power; it is its atmospheric condition.

THE SOFT ARCHITECTURE OF POWER

States do not govern primarily through force, they govern through environment. A physical environment, yes, but more importantly a symbolic one:

the calendar of holidays, the rhythm of civic rituals, the recitation of pledges, the rise of flags, the presence of official language, the invisible lines that separate "us" from "them."

These structures form a soft architecture. They shape perception as efficiently as walls shape movement.

A flag hung at the right height becomes a quiet signal of belonging. A national myth repeated often enough becomes indistinguishable from memory. A schoolbook written by anonymous hands becomes a lineage, a heritage, a map of the world as it "truly" is.

Power does not whisper, people whisper on behalf of power.

RITUAL AS THE ENGINE OF CONTINUITY

Every state invents ritual, but only mature states make ritual seem ancient.

Ritual is the mechanism by which obedience becomes desirable.

It reduces the complexity of the world to manageable symbols: the anthem, the uniform, the oath. Each is a shorthand for belonging, a small emotional hook designed to attach identity to authority.

Ritual simplifies the messy, contradictory history of power into something ceremonial, almost sacred. It converts obedience from a political act into a moral one. A patriotic gesture becomes indistinguishable from a good deed.

When ritual succeeds, power becomes a feeling.

THE EMOTIONAL GEOGRAPHY OF OBEDIENCE

Authority is most stable when it aligns itself with emotional needs.

Thus the state does not simply command, it comforts, reassures, consoles.

It promises belonging to those who fear isolation.

It promises identity to those who feel anonymous.

It promises security to those who feel fragile.

It promises order to those who fear uncertainty.

And in this way, obedience becomes a refuge.

People do not obey because they are weak, they obey because the state offers an emotional architecture that feels safer than freedom. Freedom is dizzying; it requires self-definition. Obedience offers a ready-made identity, pre-shaped and pre-approved.

A state is strongest when its people feel smaller without it.

THE BUREAUCRATIC SUBLIME

There is a strange beauty in the mechanism of the modern state, a kind of bureaucratic sublime. Its power is diffuse, distributed, anonymous. No single actor enforces it; instead, it is embedded in the process.

A form to fill out.

A line to stand in.

A document that proves your existence.

A number assigned to your life.

These artifacts of administration produce obedience without any visible coercion. The citizen complies not because they fear punishment, but because the structure feels inevitable. The bureaucratic sublime is the sensation of being inside a system too large to see, too intricate to argue with.

Here obedience is not a choice, it is the ambient logic of everyday life.

The Inheritance of Assumptions

The most powerful form of obedience is the obedience we no longer recognize as obedience, the obedience embedded in our assumptions.

We assume borders matter.

We assume nations are natural.

We assume authority is necessary.

We assume the state is the default form of civilization.

These assumptions are inheritances. They flow across generations not as commands but as culture. By the time they reach the individual, they are no longer experienced as ideology but as common sense.

Obedience becomes invisible because it appears self-evident.

WHEN OBEDIENCE BECOMES IDENTITY

The state is most stable when people stop distinguishing between obedience and self-expression.

When the citizen believes that defending the state is the same as defending themselves, disobedience becomes unthinkable.

This is the perfection of the control apparatus:

not domination, but fusion.

The state does not force you to obey; it becomes the terrain on which obedience feels natural. And once that fusion occurs, once identity and state converge, the machinery of obedience becomes self-maintaining.

The citizen polices the boundaries of their own imagination.

THE DISSOLUTION OF ALTERNATIVES

A final stage of obedience emerges when alternatives cease to appear possible. The world becomes mapped only in the vocabulary of states: nations, borders, governments, rights, citizens. The conceptual universe shrinks until the state is not merely one system of organization, it is the only imaginable one.

Power becomes reality.

Obedience becomes normalcy.

The horizon becomes a wall.

When this happens, obedience is not enforced from above, but generated from within.

Obedience is a machinery woven from emotion, ritual, narrative, identity, and inherited assumptions. It is a form of internal cartography, a mental map where the edges of thought coincide with the edges of the state.

The task of Post-State Futurism is not to reject obedience, but to reveal it; not to condemn the state, but to understand the subtle alchemy by which it becomes indistinguishable from the self.

Only then can new forms of belonging be imagined.

CHAPTER VI

The Soft Architecture of Allegiance

Allegiance is often described as loyalty, patriotism, or civic duty, yet its true structure is far subtler than any of those words suggest. Allegiance is an architecture: soft, invisible, and atmospheric, woven through the inner rooms of consciousness. Hard power compels bodies; soft power compels beliefs. And beliefs, once aligned, require no enforcement at all. They enforce themselves.

States have long understood that the most enduring form of control is not the command but the instinct, the reflexive, unexamined sense that one belongs to something larger, something unquestionable, something that stands before birth and outlasts death. Allegiance is therefore not an act but a climate, a pressure system that shapes perception even when one feels perfectly free.

This is why the modern state, despite its procedural sophistication, still invests heavily in symbols, rituals, and myths. Flags are not administrative necessities; they are psychological emulsifiers that bind individuals into a shared trance. National holidays are not moments of collective joy; they are rhythmic pulses in a larger circulatory system of identity. School civics lessons do not teach facts; they cultivate sentiment. And sentiment, once rooted in childhood, becomes as durable as bone.

Yet the architecture is soft because it does not declare itself. Its beams are feelings, not instructions. Its walls are unspoken assumptions. Its roof is the sky of inherited narratives: the stories one never chose to believe but believes nonetheless.

THE INTERIORIZATION OF THE STATE

By the time an individual reaches adulthood, the state has already been absorbed into the structure of the self. One does not simply live within a nation; one carries it inside like a phantom organ, a symbolic appendix of belonging.

The locus of power has shifted. It no longer rests in external structures of law, bureaucracy, or surveillance. It rests in the interiorization of duty, the normalization of expectation, the quiet adherence to inherited frameworks of meaning.

This inward shift is what allows the state to maintain stability even in moments of crisis. Revolutions often fail not because the people cannot seize power, but because they cannot yet relinquish the invisible architecture they grew up inside. The state collapses in the streets long before it collapses in the imagination.

The deepest prisons are not made of stone; they are made of metaphors.

THE ORNAMENTATION OF COLLECTIVE IDENTITY

Every society produces a gallery of symbolic ornaments designed to reinforce the soft architecture of allegiance. History is compressed into founding myths that read as moral fables. National narratives smooth over the brutality of origins. Heroic archetypes sanctify obedience. Unity is rehearsed through ritual. Geography itself is elevated into sacred truth.

These ornaments serve a dual purpose. They provide emotional texture to belonging, and they obscure the material foundations of state power: the labor extracted, the compliance demanded, the limits imposed. The more elaborate the ornamentation becomes, the less visible the machinery beneath it.

In this sense, the state survives by enchanting its own citizens. It casts coherence over chaos, meaning over randomness, and destiny over what are ultimately accidents of geography. These spells feel like comfort. Their function is containment.

THE SOFT CAGE OF INHERITED MEANING

Allegiance often masquerades as pride. But pride is rarely spontaneous; it is cultivated. The soft cage of inherited meaning is built gradually and gently, through the rituals of childhood:

the hand over the heart

the pledge recited by millions

the anthem performed at the threshold of every public gathering

the maps that draw clean borders over centuries of conflict

the textbooks that begin with noble intentions, never with syndicate origins

In this sense, the state does not merely want obedience; it seeks continuity. It wants its narratives to be carried forward not as instruction but as inheritance, not as doctrine but as affection.

A citizen who obeys the law is useful.

A citizen who defends the law emotionally is invaluable.

The Emotionalization of Authority

Many political theorists have described power as rational or strategic, but allegiance reveals power to be fundamentally emotional. People do not mourn for governments, they mourn for symbols. They do not bleed for tax codes, they bleed for flags. They do not suffer for constitutions, they suffer for imagined communities bound by sentiment, story, and sacrifice.

The state's most enduring power is not its monopoly on violence, but its monopoly on meaning. It offers citizens a story in which being governed feels like being part of something sacred.

Meaning anesthetizes domination.

THE CRACKS IN THE ARCHITECTURE

Soft architectures crack in subtle ways, often beginning at the edges where reality diverges too sharply from myth. These cracks manifest as disillusionment, irony, cynicism, or the sudden awareness that belonging was never a choice but an inheritance.

When these cracks widen, citizens begin to see the architecture for what it is: not destiny, but design.

At first this realization is destabilizing. The warm embrace of inherited identity becomes a draft of cold air. The emotional scaffolding that once held everything in place begins to feel like an imposition. But through these cracks enters clarity, the first light of post-state consciousness.

The goal is not to reject all belonging. Humans need belonging. But to choose belonging freely is different from receiving it through the quiet coercion of generational conditioning.

The future begins at the moment when allegiance becomes elective rather than inherited.

TOWARD THE DECONSTRUCTION OF ALLEGIANCE.

As technological networks expand, mobility increases, and hybrid identities proliferate, the soft architecture of allegiance begins to buckle. People form communities across distance, collaborate across borders, and imagine themselves outside the limits of geography. The state loses its monopoly on meaning.

In this transitional era, allegiance becomes unbundled. Individuals no longer feel tethered to a single collective identity. Their loyalty shifts across multiple domains: creative, cultural, professional, philosophical. The self becomes nodal long before civilization does.

The architecture dissolves from within.

THE THRESHOLD OF POST-STATE BELONGING

What emerges is not isolation, but plurality. The human need for belonging remains, but finds new forms:

Smaller, intentional, affinity-based, value-aligned communities

Not defined by land, but by purpose

Not inherited, but chosen

At this threshold, allegiance ceases to be a soft chain and becomes a soft bridge, an opening toward a civilization in which identity is no longer the residue of borders but the expression of freedom.

In this transition, the poetic and the political converge. The human being awakens not as a subject of a state, but as a participant in a world of fluid, voluntary associations.

Chapter VI closes with this recognition:

What we once called allegiance was often only habituation.

What we will one day call allegiance will be something else entirely:

A conscious, creative act.

CHAPTER VII

The Birth of the Political Self

The political self is not the individual. It is the individual after being read by power. It is the human being rendered into legible shapes, measured, registered, counted, taxed, guided, and positioned as a node within a vast administrative constellation.

No one is born with a political self. It is constructed through the long apprenticeship of growing up inside a state. The political self is not who we are. It is who the state requires us to become.

THE INDIVIDUAL AS UNREADABLE ORIGIN

Before the state inscribes itself, the human being exists as a horizon of potential. Identity emerges from experience, feeling, relationship, curiosity, and immediate life with others, rather than from any external classification. Children demonstrate this condition with particular clarity. They belong first to the world, not to the nation. They invent borders that are temporary and imaginative, dissolving them as soon as they lose interest. They form alliances through affinity rather than obligation. Their authority is emotional rather than institutional.

This pre-political existence is not merely a feature of childhood. It is the latent condition of the human being prior to the imposition of state form.

THE STATE'S FIRST TASK: COMPRESSION

The state narrows the human horizon. It compresses the breadth of being into a single alignment: membership within a polity. To accomplish this, it constructs a controlled grammar of identity. The individual is rendered as a citizen, a demographic unit, a legal subject, a taxpayer, a draftable body, a jurisdiction-bound entity. These terms do not describe a person. They delimit permission and constraint.

Through this grammar, the state determines who may move and who must remain, who may speak and who must remain silent, who may vote, who may work, who may be punished, and who may be protected, and under what conditions each applies. The political self that results is not a personality or a belief system. It is an architecture of legibility.

RITUAL AS THE ENGINE OF POLITICAL FORMATION

The state does not imprint identity through force alone. It relies on repetition, enacted softly, persistently, and ceremonially. Ritual does not require belief to function. It requires only participation. Graduation ceremonies, pledge recitations, anthem singing, border crossings, voting booths, and holiday parades are not symbolic extras; they are the means by which the state rehearses itself through the bodies of its citizens.

Through ritual, the political self becomes embodied memory. Gestures are learned before they are understood. Expectations are absorbed before they are questioned. Even those who resist the state rarely escape the choreography that ritual has etched into posture, timing, and reflex. The body remembers what the mind attempts to refuse.

LANGUAGE AS A TERRITORIAL CLAIM

The political self is also shaped through linguistic conditioning. Words such as nation, patriotism, security, law and order, citizen, alien, border, and homeland do not function as neutral descriptors. They operate as territorial claims on thought. Each term carries assumptions about belonging, legitimacy, threat, and authority that precede any conscious use.

Even dissent often borrows this vocabulary without noticing the structures embedded within it. Language contains invisible enclosures. A person may believe they are speaking freely while remaining inside a linguistic architecture constructed centuries before their birth.

ADMINISTRATIVE IDENTITY AND THE FICTION OF SAMENESS

The political self is mass-produced. It is engineered for populations large enough to require processing at scale. The state does not treat millions as unique beings, but as functionally substitutable units. From this necessity emerges the administrative person, an identity composed of records, entries, and identifiers that stand in for the individual.

To the state, these abstractions become more real than the human they reference. The passport, the census entry, the identification number, the legal persona, the health record, and the financial profile are legible in ways the individual is not. The political self is therefore a useful fiction: a simplified mask that allows the machinery of governance to operate. The real self is too complex, too irregular, to govern efficiently.

THE INTERNALIZATION OF BORDERS

The most consequential achievement of the political self is the internal border. Long before boundaries are encountered as lines on a map, they are carried inward as assumptions about what may be said, where one belongs, what kinds of lives are permissible, which strangers inspire suspicion, and which authorities feel beyond challenge. Borders migrate from geography into psychology.

The state succeeds most completely when it no longer needs to enforce the boundary directly, because the citizen has learned to enforce it internally. At that point, the line holds without patrol.

THE POLITICAL SELF AS SUBSTITUTE FOR COMMUNITY

In the absence of tribal intimacy, familial sovereignty, or village-scale interdependence, the modern state offers a surrogate belonging. Citizenship becomes the mass-produced replacement for community. It is thin enough to scale, symbolic enough to unify, abstract enough to apply to millions, and emotional enough to feel reassuring.

Yet this belonging is fragile. It is sustained less by connection than by anxiety: fear of outsiders, fear of disorder, fear of meaninglessness. The political self experiences security only when the state's boundaries appear stable. When those boundaries waver, the sense of belonging collapses with them.

THE CRISIS OF THE POLITICAL SELF IN THE TWENTY-FIRST CENTURY

Globalization, migration, digital life, hybrid identity, cosmopolitan practice, and creative mobility destabilize the political self. Increasingly, individuals resist governance by territorial logic alone. Affiliations form independently of geography. Identity diversifies beyond national narrative. The political self begins to fracture as the individual re-expands.

Within this fracture, a different horizon becomes visible. The post-state condition appears not as an ideology, but as a response to lived complexity that no longer fits inherited frames.

THE UNMAKING OF THE POLITICAL SELF

To move beyond the state, the political self must be disassembled deliberately and without rupture. This is not erasure. It is restoration. The aim is not to eliminate political identity, but to release it from the state's exclusive ownership.

What emerges is a shift in posture rather than a negation of self. The individual becomes a node rather than a subject, a participant rather than a citizen, a collaborator rather than a demographic unit. Affiliation becomes a choice instead of an inheritance.

The unmaking of the political self is therefore not an endpoint. It is the first act of post-state becoming.

TOWARD THE POST-POLITICAL SELF

The post-political self is not without community, norms, or responsibility. What it rejects is compulsory belonging. It attaches itself instead to voluntary structures, to nodes and fluid collectivities organized around meaning rather than geography.

In a post-state condition, selfhood is no longer shaped by territory, but by alignment. It is formed not through inherited narrative, but through chosen purpose. Legibility to the state gives way to self-determination as the organizing principle of identity.

CHAPTER VIII

The Ethics of Presence in a World Structured by Power

ETHICS AFTER THE STATE

There comes a point in any inquiry into the nature of the state when description is no longer sufficient. Analysis alone risks becoming a form of paralysis, an endless circling of mechanisms, histories, and structures. A theory that limits itself to illumination can drift into complicity. Knowledge becomes another mode of obedience when it refuses to cross the boundary into ethics.

Post-State Futurism therefore reaches a necessary question: what does it mean to live ethically inside a system built on containment, inheritance, and the domestication of perception? What does it mean to act within a structure that predates us, shapes us, and claims to speak on our behalf?

This chapter offers no commandments. It seeks instead to unfold the shape of an ethical posture appropriate to beings born into a world already organized for them, its lines drawn, its rituals rehearsed, its categories waiting. It begins with the self, moves outward into the world, and ends at the horizon beyond the state.

THE FRACTURE AT THE CENTER OF MODERN ETHICS

Modern ethical life is compromised by a foundational contradiction. Individuals are taught to imagine themselves as autonomous moral agents while living inside structures designed to regulate their possibilities long before they can name them. The state demands obedience while rewarding conformity. Liberalism celebrates individuality while organizing life through mass institutions. Democracy promises voice while filtering it through layers of representation and symbolic participation.

Ethical life is therefore shaped by an invisible fracture: a self encouraged to feel free within a world meticulously arranged to limit that freedom. Most people attempt to resolve this contradiction by retreating into private virtue, emphasizing kindness, decency, or restraint. Yet the state does not measure virtue. It measures compliance.

Any ethics adequate to the present must therefore begin with clarity rather than consolation. To be born into a state is to inherit a system that predetermines the conditions of one's ethical life. This recognition is not fatalism. It is orientation.

THE ETHICS OF SEEING CLEARLY

Before action comes perception. In a world designed by the state, the most radical ethical act is to see the design itself. This means noticing how borders present themselves as natural facts, how identities bind themselves to narratives authored elsewhere, how ritual bypasses reason to install memory, how belonging is packaged as loyalty, and how obedience is rehearsed until it becomes reflex.

Clarity is not rebellion. It is presence. It is the refusal to allow inherited narratives to think in place of the self. This ethical posture does not demand the rejection of institutions, but it does refuse unconscious participation within them. The first task of ethical life is therefore not resistance, but awakening.

THE ETHICS OF NON-DOMINATION

Post-State Futurism does not advance an anarchic ethics, nor an ethic of universal negation. Its center of gravity lies in the principle of non-domination: the refusal to participate in, normalize, or reproduce systems that require the coerced narrowing of human possibility.

Under this principle, loyalty cannot be ethically demanded by structures to which individuals never meaningfully consented. Human mobility cannot be morally constrained by accidents of geography. Identity cannot be reduced to birthplace without violence. Power that relies on the unconscious reproduction of obedience cannot be justified as order.

Non-domination does not imply withdrawal from all systems. It requires continuous evaluation of whether participation is freely chosen or structurally compelled. If existence itself is conditional upon obedience, then life is not ethical but managed. Constraint is unavoidable. Unquestioned constraint is not.

THE ETHICS OF THE VOLUNTARY BELONGING

The state presents citizenship as the foundation of belonging. Yet belonging precedes the state. Human connection predates every border ever drawn. An ethics of voluntary belonging recognizes that attachment is deepest when it is chosen, that identity is truest when it is not inherited by force, and that community is most authentic when it arises from shared meaning rather than shared jurisdiction.

To belong ethically is to refuse the reduction of identity to territory. It is to accept that one's most vital communities may not be sanctioned by passports, flags, or national mythologies. Voluntary belonging is not an abandonment of society. It is a re-centering of social life around intention rather than inheritance.

THE ETHICS OF REFUSING THE INVISIBLE CAGE

The most insidious restriction imposed by the modern state is not external but internal. It operates upon imagination. When a society teaches that life must unfold within fixed economic, geographic, political, and cultural boundaries, entire futures are foreclosed before they can be perceived.

To live ethically is to cultivate the capacity to imagine otherwise. This imagination is not escapism. It is resistance to mental captivity. Ethical life requires permeability to visions beyond the inherited horizon, refusal of limits that merely feel inevitable, and protection of the inner landscape from colonization by collective myth. If the state functions as a macro-syndicate of power, imagination becomes the micro-rebellion of the self.

THE ETHICS OF TRANSITION

Post-State Futurism does not call for rupture. Civilizations do not transform overnight. Identities untangle slowly. New forms emerge within the shell of the old. Ethical transformation is therefore transitional rather than revolutionary.

To live ethically between worlds is to weaken unconscious loyalties that feed coercive systems, to build alternative forms of community grounded in choice, to participate selectively in institutions while supporting only their humane functions, and to refuse the equation of obedience with virtue. It is to strengthen networks that resist territorial containment while preparing inner life for a world not yet fully realized.

Ethics becomes the architecture of transition, the scaffolding of a future quietly assembled within the present.

THE ETHICAL HORIZON BEYOND THE STATE

States rarely end through collapse. They end through irrelevance. The ethical task of the present is to midwife the forms of life that will render territorial power obsolete. This horizon points toward voluntary nodes of community, distributed cultural meaning, post-territorial identity, mobility as a human condition, governance without inherited coercion, and affiliation without borders.

Ethics does not seek to destroy the state. It seeks to outgrow it. The highest ethical act is therefore not rebellion, but replacement: the steady emergence of ways of living that make the cage unnecessary until it dissolves from lack of purpose.

This is the direction toward which Post-State Futurism moves, an ethics expansive enough to imagine a human future no longer defined by territorial power, and intimate enough to guide the self through the long corridor of transition.

CHAPTER IX

The Threshold of the Post-State Mind

There is a point in every long-running system: biological, ecological, social, when continuity becomes exhaustion. The state, as we inherited it, stands at such a point. It does not collapse outwardly; it erodes inwardly. Not through rebellion, but through irrelevance. Not through fire, but through forgetting. The twentieth century framed the state as eternal; the twenty-first reveals its seams.

The threshold of the post-state mind begins where inherited loyalties begin to loosen, quietly, almost imperceptibly. These shifts are never dramatic; they do not appear on news broadcasts or in legislative chambers. They occur inside the private architecture of consciousness. They occur when an individual recognizes that the state is not the container of their life but simply one of the forces passing through it.

This realization is not an act of rebellion. It is an act of remembering: remembering that human association, collaboration, meaning, creativity, and belonging are older than the state and more enduring than any border.

THE SOFT DISSOLUTION OF THE FRAME

The decline of an idea rarely occurs through argument. It happens through disuse. Through the gradual dissipation of its emotional charge. Through the quiet recognition that its promises no longer animate the future. The state's claim to inevitability weakens not because people oppose it, but because they outgrow it.

This soft dissolution is already underway.

People live transnationally while still anchored administratively. They form communities that are invisible to census officials. They develop economic ties that run perpendicular to borders. They become fluent in cultures other than the one printed on their passport. The psyche drifts before institutions do.

The state continues its rituals: elections, ceremonies, patriotic anniversaries, even as fewer people feel shaped by them. These rituals become hollow recitations of a grand narrative whose chapters no longer match lived experience. The frame remains, but the meaning leaks out.

THE STATE AFTER NECESSITY

When a structure persists beyond its necessity, it becomes ornamental. Much like old religious institutions that persist long after belief has waned, the state begins to operate on symbolic momentum.

It still governs, but governance becomes less central to the lives of those on whom it relies.

It still collects taxes, but taxation begins to feel like the maintenance cost of a legacy system.

It still claims authority, but the authority feels curated, staged, and increasingly performative.

The state becomes a familiar interface with an emptying core.

Its greatest threat is not overthrow but obsolescence.

The Reappearance of the Human.

What emerges in this quiet vacuum is not chaos but possibility.

The collapse of an overgrown framework reveals the contours of the things it once concealed: the voluntary, the creative, the relational, the communal, the improvisational, the human.

The human reappears after centuries of being subsumed into the category of "citizen," which flattened differences, silenced complexities, and reduced individuality to a manageable administrative unit. Citizenship is replaced by participation. Belonging becomes something one does, not something one inherits.

The post-state mind does not flee the state; it simply recognizes that human possibility exceeds it.

THE QUIET BIRTH OF THE NODAL CONSCIOUSNESS

Every major transformation begins as a change in interior weather.

The nodal intelligence that will shape the next civilization begins first as a subtle redirection of emotional loyalty, then as an intellectual reframing of identity, and finally as a practical shift in the way individuals choose to organize their lives.

Before nodal society appears in institutions, it appears in intuitions.

People begin to sense that their true affiliations lie elsewhere: in craft, in culture, in shared imaginative worlds, in distributed creative networks, in communities of meaning that cross borders without noticing them.

The nation becomes an administrative address.

The node becomes a home.

CROSSING THE THRESHOLD

The threshold of the post-state mind is not a political event. It is a psychological maturation. It begins with a recognition: that creative life is not a national asset, that freedom is not bestowed by the state but bounded by it, that identity is not anchored to territory, and that purpose is not confined by inherited loyalties.

The state was a solution to a specific historical condition, one shaped by scarcity, fragility, slow communication, and the necessity of fixed defense. That condition no longer defines the present. To cross the threshold is not to abandon the state, but to stop imagining it as the container of the human future.

TOWARD THE HORIZON OF BOOK II

Book I has traced the long roots of state formation, the architecture of obedience, the domestication of populations, and the first emergence of post-state consciousness. But standing at a threshold is not the same as crossing it.

As Book II unfolds, the inquiry shifts from the genealogy of the state to the contours of what follows it. Attention turns toward the ethics, architectures, and lived realities of nodal civilization, not as abstraction, but as practice.

Book I therefore ends without a conclusion. It ends with an opening. The post-state mind begins as a realization, settles into reorientation, and, over time, crystallizes into a world.

Acknowledgments

My thanks go to the varied influences that informed this work: the independent force of Washington, DC's punk culture, the structural rigor of life in a region shaped by federal institutions and the ambient pressure of inherited political narratives, and the collaborators and colleagues of Corgan Studio whose perspectives broadened my understanding of systems and design. I also acknowledge the artists and thinkers who helped me see structure and narrative in new ways. I am grateful to offer this work as a tool for questioning and reimagining the frameworks that shape our world.

Also in the Post-State Futurism Trilogy

Book I: Foundations of Post-State Futurism

Book II: The Post-State Imagination

Book III: The Post-State Condition

About the Author

Jason Corgan Brown is an award-winning filmmaker and design consultant whose work spans cinema, immersive media, conceptual environments, and urban development. Raised in the Washington, DC area, surrounded by federal institutions and shaped by the independent ethos of the local punk scene, he developed an early sensitivity to structure, perception, and the forces that shape civic life. Through Corgan Studio, he has contributed to major studio productions and international design initiatives, working across narrative, space, and systems. Book I of the Post-State Futurism trilogy is his first full articulation of a framework years in development, combining artistic practice with structural and philosophical inquiry.